I0036943

INDIE AUTHOR MAGAZINE

HELLO AND WELCOME!

I'm Indie Annie, and I'm thrilled you're reading this gorgeous full-color version of IAM. Did you know that you can also access all the information, education, and inspiration in our app? It's available on both the iOS App Store and Google Play. And for those that prefer to listen to me read articles, you can pop over to Spotify or our website. Happy Reading!

X

IndieAuthorMagazine.com

Download on the App Store

GET IT ON Google Play

Spotify

PLOT POINTS

PLOT POINTS

Plotting a Book vs. a Screenplay

Writing with Chronic Illness

10 Tips for Newsletter Content

Growth in the Indie Author Industry

The ABCs of Publishing Picture Books

You Go Faster When You Go Slower

INDIE AUTHOR MAGAZINE

Volume 2 · Issue 4 · April 2022

This Issue's Featured Author: RICARDO FAYET

ON THE COVER

INDiE
AUTHOR MAGAZINE

PUBLISHER
Chelle Honiker

CREATIVE DIRECTOR
Alice Briggs

CONSULTING EDITOR
Nicole Schroeder

COPY EDITOR
Lisa Thompson

WRITERS
Angela Archer
Elaine Bateman
Patricia Carr
Laurel Decher
Fatima Fayez
Gill Fernley
Greg Fishbone
Remy Flagg
Chrishaun Keller-Hanna
Jac Harmon
Marion Hermannsen

WRITERS
Kasia Lasinska
Bre Lockhart
Anne Lown
Sìne Màiri MacDougall
Merri Maywether
Lasairiona McMaster
Susan Odev
Clare Sager
Nicole Schroeder
Emilia Zeeland

PUBLISHER
Athenia Creative
6820 Apus Dr.
Sparks, NV, 89436 USA
775.298.1925

ISSN 2768-7880 (online)–ISSN 2768-7872 (print)

The publication, authors, and contributors reserve their rights in regards to copyright of their work. No part of this work covered by the copyright may be reproduced or copied in any form or by any means without the written consent of the publisher. All copyrighted work was reproduced with the permission of the owner.

Reasonable care is taken to ensure that *Indie Author Magazine* articles and other information on the website are up to date and as accurate as possible, at the time of publication, but no responsibility can be taken by *Indie Author Magazine* for any errors or omissions contained herein. Furthermore, *Indie Author Magazine* takes no responsibility for any losses, damages, or distress resulting from adherence to any information made available through this publication. The opinions expressed are those of the authors and do not necessarily reflect the views of *Indie Author Magazine*.

PLAN YOUR BOOKS THE WAY YOU THINK

Plottr

Outline faster, plot smarter, and turbocharge your productivity today with the #1 visual book planning software for writers.

USE CODE "IAM" FOR 10% OFF

https://writelink.to/plottr

From the Publisher

I have always seen IAM as an extension of the larger indie author community, born out of a group of international writers who met daily via Zoom and shared what they were doing to climb the mountain of success. Beyond the business chat between sprints, we also became bonded friends.

There would not be a magazine without the unconditional support, generosity, and genuine affection we've developed for one another.

And while I know it's **incredibly** special, I realize that it's not singular.

In the middle of a global phenomenon, authors around the world have formed and strengthened communities via Zoom, Slack, Discord, Clubhouse, TikTok, and other social media channels.

Every day, new authors are connecting with experienced authors and are learning from one another and supporting each other's careers and lives.

This magazine was born out of those communities, and it's why we work to amplify as many resources as possible, including books, software, websites, blogs, tools, and podcasts.

As I look at our industry today, I think of the African proverb, "If you want to go fast, go alone; but if you want to go far, go together."

As IAM Turns One, We're Adding Something New

Later this summer, we'll have several days of interactive presentations designed to help indie authors learn and evaluate the plethora of technology choices. We'll ask the questions you would ask of the software providers, and we'll break the geek-speak down into understandable language.

We call it the Author Tech Summit.

I'm excited to see ways we can help share more resources with the indie author community. It's a particular passion of mine to see authors find innovative ways to learn and grow their careers.

If you'd like to learn more about ATS, we've built a dedicated website: https://authortechsummit.com.

I hope we see you there, as we all "go together."

To Your Success,
Chelle
Publisher
Indie Author Magazine

LastPass®

Auto-pilot for all your passwords

Writelink.to/lastpass

Dear Indie Annie,

How do I know I'm good enough? Writing a book takes time and effort. What if my novel is utter rubbish? I'll have wasted all that time and effort.

Wasting Time in Wabasca

DEAR WABASCA,

I do love a time waster.

In fact, like many writers, I like nothing better than to spend my day researching little-known facts on the internet.

And your question prompted me to check the population of Wasbasca on the Alberta Open Government Website. You probably already know this but I was fascinated to discover that the population of your hometown stands at 166, only because your little community welcomed another bundle of joy this past year, bless their tiny cotton socks, or you would still be resting happily at a majestic 165.

Also, I learned that the local airport serves a wider population of roughly ten times that amount across several Indian reserves. The name "Wasbasca" derives from the Cree word for White Grass and the river that runs through the territory.

I could go on, but I won't.

To answer your question, "Have I just been wasting my time?"

Possibly.

But, then again, I could argue (and I will) that, well, thanks to the beautiful people at IAM, I am actually being paid to read, consider, research, and respond to your question. While many reading this response will agree that I have totally wasted my time and IAM has blown their hard-won dollars on an old hack trying to justify her meager paycheck, others will understand exactly what I am trying to illuminate here with this quite brilliant analogy.

Everything can be a waste of time if you consider it to be so.

And every-**thing that isn't a waste of time takes effort.**

Do you consider honing your craft

Need help from your favorite Indie Aunt?
Ask Dear Indie Annie a question at
IndieAnnie@indieauthormagazine.com

a worthwhile activity? Do you want to be a great writer, or is this a passing fancy? Do you want to create stories that take people away from the tedium of their humdrum existence? Or perhaps you have a wealth of knowledge that will transform their lives when expertly packaged. Maybe what you write will be deemed by many to be the ramblings of a romantic wannabe with zero talent, or perhaps your particular brand of pulp fiction will develop a cult following that will spawn a merchandising frenzy across the globe.

The real question is, ***do you think it is worth the time and effort*** to find out?

If your answer to that question is yes, then the ultimate acid test of whether you have wasted your time and effort will lie in what happens next. How will you measure success?

What, in your mind, will determine if it was worth it?

For many, it is the process: writing a story with a beginning, a middle, and an end. For some, it will be when they hit publish; others, when they hold the printed proof copy in their hands. Then it could be your first page read on KDP or the first hundred books sold. Maybe it will be your first five-star review that wasn't from a friend or family member. For the really sadistic, it will be the honor badge of that one-star review. Then you will know you have made it.

How much do *you* need?

For me, it's a simple trifecta: to be a New York Times bestseller, get that elusive movie deal, and have my own rabid fan hold me captive in the mountains while I bring her favorite character back to life.

As to the question, are you good enough, yada, yada? There really is only one way to find out. In the words of Arthur Wellesley, Duke of Wellington, "Publish and be damned."

He meant that he didn't care for his reputation, and my beloved one, neither should you.

You will still have achieved what many merely dream of doing. It may be a hard fight to get there, but I am sure the Duke of Wellington would agree: It is a battle worth entering.

Happy writing,
Indie Annie X

10 TIPS FOR
NEWSLETTER CONTENT

Aside from book updates, newsletter swaps, and group promos, you might struggle to keep coming up with fresh content ideas for your newsletter. You will need to take time to figure out what your audience responds to and to build a relationship with them so you learn what makes them click on links, reply to you, and ultimately buy your books.

That constant feeling of needing to find content can make newsletter writing feel like a painful task, much like a trip to the dentist for a root canal. But nailing your email marketing game is important for sustained growth and success. So while it may feel painful now, your future self will thank you for your current efforts.

As ever, we here at IAM HQ have your back. Here are our top ten tips for finding content ideas.

1 START WITH A GOAL IN MIND

Searching for content ideas without an end goal in mind is like going fishing without a rod. In a vast sea of information, ideas, and well-meaning advice from other authors, you can get lost and overwhelmed quickly. The best thing to do is to stop. Pause for a minute. Think about what you want your newsletter to achieve and start from there.

Just like writing a scene in your novel, think about what you want your reader to know, feel, and do after reading your newsletter. Do you want to make them chuckle or encourage them, or do you want to educate them about a specific topic? You might want to promote your social media channel, so you'd create a post on said channel, then tantalize them with a hook, pique their natural curiosity, and direct them to that particular post.

By setting a goal and narrowing down your search before looking for ideas, you'll save yourself a lot of time.

Pro Tip: Different types of content elicit different responses, but typically content that results in making readers feel happy and inspired tends to be shared the most.

2 FOLLOW THE NEWS

We have access to so much information these days, and nothing moves faster than the news (and the Twitter feed). Randomly checking the news could easily pull you into a rabbit hole. So use websites like Feedly (https://feedly.com) or Inoreader (https://inoreader.com) to define your interests and relevant publications and combine them into one easy-to-read newsfeed. Both these services offer free plans that should be sufficient to meet your needs.

3 LOOK FOR TRENDING HASHTAGS

Similarly to checking the newsfeed, you can easily find the hottest topics and trending conversations by following trending hashtags. Staying current and relevant can seem hard and time-consuming. But if you're smart about it, by using sites like hashtagify (https://hashtagify.me), you'll save time and build your brand with on-trend topics.

4 FORUMS

Another way to find out what people are talking about (and stay relevant) is to take a look at forums like Reddit (https://reddit.com), Quora (https://quora.com), and other similar sites. Look for subreddits in your genre or broader topics relating to your niche.

Pro Tip: Narrow down your Google search to only include discussion forums. We're all about saving time, and you don't want to be scrolling through the plethora of results a general Google search will throw up. If you use Google Chrome, you can hit the discussion tab—it's a small tab underneath the search. If you're on Google, just follow your search question with this text: inurl:reddit|forum|viewthread|viewtopic|showthread|showtopic|"index.php?topic" and Google will show you discussion threads.

5 ASK YOUR READERS

Asking your readers is as simple as it sounds. You can do a survey or poll or ask for a quick reply. Just be aware that readers might tell you what they think you want to hear. A whole bunch of psychology is attached to that statement and reasons why people do that, but if people think your ego is on the line, then they'll give you fluffy feel-good compliments. So think carefully about the questions you pose and how you pose them, then just be prepared to read between the lines.

Pro Tip: Recommended reading: *The Mom Test* by Rob Fitzpatrick and *Ask* by Ryan Levesue are both great reads if you want to dig deeper into understanding your audience and asking the right questions.

6 ANALYZE PAST EMAILS

If you've been sending emails regularly, you'll have a solid history of data to review and assess. Take a look at past campaigns, compare subject lines, and evaluate the content and or theme within that campaign. Ask how well the subject line correlated to the content and how it affected the outcome. What type of content got your readers to take an action (usually a link click)? Which emails had the most engagement? Compare those to the ones that got the least. See if you can see a common theme.

Don't go mad here or go back over the lifetime of your newsletter. Just look long enough to pick up on any trends. If you email every two weeks, you might only go back over the last three months. If you email monthly, you might want to review the last six to nine months. Pick a time interval that makes sense.

7 SEASONAL CALENDARS

Use holidays and seasonal events to your advantage, especially if you're running a promo and can relate it to a national or international holiday or awareness week. You could, if the connection is strong enough, write a press release and send it to a newspaper for even more coverage. Then write about that in your newsletter. Awareness Days.com (https://awarenessdays.com/awareness-days-calendar) is a handy site for finding out about national and international awareness days/weeks/months.

8 LOOK FOR SMALL STUFF

First and foremost, we are authors. Storytelling is what we do. But we forget to write about ourselves. We hold back because we don't want to give too much of ourselves away, or maybe we don't think anyone will be interested, or we're looking for big events that might interest our readers.

The truth is, you can tell little stories, everyday tidbits to help to build a bond with your readers. You don't have to tell them about big, deep, personal stuff. It might be about unexpected news or how you met a man in a coffee shop that looked exactly like one of the characters in your upcoming release. The little things that happen in our lives and the way we react to them help our readers bond with us—just like they would with a character in your book.

9 BE OPEN

Look for out-of-the-box ideas. Schedule a brain-dumping session. Put your reader at the center with a statement like, "My readers are into historical romance and often say they were born in the wrong century." Then mind-map what they might value, what they want from life/love, what they hate, and what problems they might have. Note any ideas that come to you and use these to direct the theme or topic of your newsletter.

Pro Tip: Something magical happens to our subconscious when we decide to become an author. You start seeing ideas and angles for stories everywhere. The same can happen with your search for content ideas. If you're really stuck, think of a goal, go for a walk, do something creative, or try a new project, and let your subconscious do its work. We can easily get bogged down by the thought that we constantly have to provide value and be entertaining, which can cloud our thinking.

10 ROUNDUPS

If you're really stuck, you could try roundups. Do a top ten list of your favorite books, songs, podcasts, or movies; your most popular social media posts; your top ten most mortifying moments in life; top ten crushes; or a list of real-life events, situations, or people that influenced your current novel. These kinds of lists are great content because they're shareable and strong conversation starters, and you can easily repurpose them for social media posts. ■

Angela Archer

Ricardo Fayet, the Friendly Face of Reedsy

As co-founder of Reedsy, Ricardo Fayet is a familiar and much-respected face in the indie publishing world. The company was formed in 2014 to curate editing and design services. Ricardo explains that its core purpose is the same now as it was then: "to provide a safe place where authors could find some of the world's best editors, cover designers, illustrators, book marketers, website designers, ghostwriters, translators, [and/or] pretty much anyone any author would need to hire at any point throughout their writing career."

A lot of work goes into ensuring that the freelancers listed in their marketplace are the best. Ricardo told us, "I think what makes it really special is that we accept less than 5 percent of the freelancers who apply to be on our marketplace. It's very curated. We pay a lot of attention. We put a lot of manual work into vetting the people who are in our marketplace to make sure that any professional whom you can hire on Reedsy is going to be a properly accomplished professional and an expert in their field."

While Ricardo didn't want to give away their secret processes for assessing freelancers, he did share that their profiles are similar to Linkedin, where the candidate lists their work experience and provides an overview of the jobs they've worked in and the services

> The company was formed in 2014 to curate editing and design services.

He's also the author of a nonfiction book called *How to Market a Book*.

they want to offer. "The most important part is the Gallery for designers, which lets us know exactly what type of books they've worked on in the past. That's generally the section we review the most, and we have the strictest criteria on."

If a freelancer wants to work with Reedsy, they might need more than five years of experience in their field; it will vary from one service to another. But they generally require traditional publishing experience for editors. That means they work (or have worked) at any of the Big Five or at a well-known independent publisher. They confirm all this with background checks.

The process for vetting literary translators involves double-checking that they are listed as literary translators and verifying all the books that they mentioned in a portfolio. They carry out a lot of manual background checks to ensure that the professionals on receipt are who they say they are and have done what they say they've done. If they meet the criteria and they pass a background check, only then will they be added to the marketplace.

DO REEDSY'S GHOSTWRITERS WRITE OUTLINES?

Ricardo confirmed that some of Reedsy's ghostwriters do write outlines. "Most of our ghostwriters specialize in nonfiction, but we've got quite a few fiction ones as well. And when they write a fiction book, just like any writer, they're going to start with an outline, or a

plot can be more or less detailed. So yes, you can hire a ghostwriter to come up with an outline based on a story idea or genre. You can definitely have them do that."

Ricardo isn't just a curator of high-quality services to the author industry. He's also the author of a nonfiction book called *How to Market a Book*. He shared his process.

"It was a bit of an uncommon process because I was trying to write a book for a while. I tried to motivate myself, but I could never really find the time and motivation. So instead what I did is, I launched a weekly marketing newsletter around three years ago, which I tried to send out every Thursday. That forced me to write between five hundred and a thousand words every week, which is not much. But over the weeks and over the years, it piled up into massive, maybe eighty-thousand-word documents. When I thought I'd covered pretty much all the topics, all the big topics that I could think about, marketing-wise, I thought I should really put them together into a book because I had all this material. I constantly had people from the newsletter ask me about past issues, so I thought, it's much easier for me to put all this into a book and send them the link to a book."

Instead of starting from an outline, Ricardo started with a bunch of different newsletters. He put them together to create the outline using an ebook editor tool. "Basically, I copy-and-pasted all the newsletters into chapters. I created different parts to group the chapters together. I created the outline based on the material that I had, then I filled in the blanks. Some of it was outdated, and I had to write transitions, but I found it much easier to complete the book once it was in order.

"This was achieved using Reedsy Book Editor's writing and formatting tool. I used it for outlining as well because you can drag and drop the chapters in the sidebar, which I think you can do in other writing programs as well. But since that one was free and I happen to be a founder of the company, I thought I was going to use that one."

DO YOU HAVE THE WRITING BUG? DO YOU WANT TO WRITE AGAIN?

Ricardo continued, "I created a series page on Amazon with this book, and I called it the first one in the Reedsy Marketing Guide. So I kind of committed to writing the next one. I should have something on Amazon ads by the summer [of 2022].

"What I found is that since the ebook is free, it doesn't have as much exposure, maybe as a paid book, that would sell quite well. So I want to put a paid book out there, not so that we make money on it, but so that it's in the paid list and it can have visibility

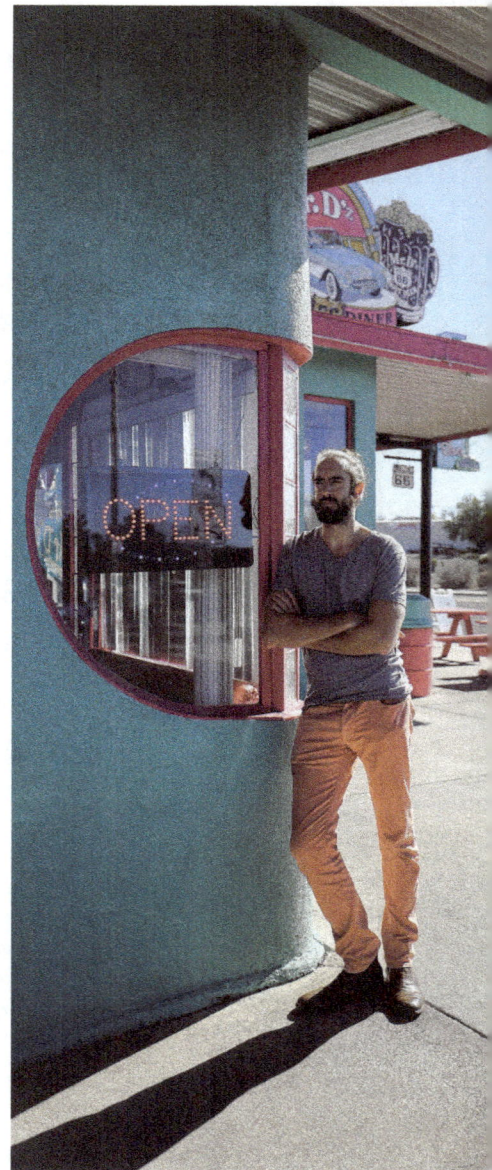

> The indie author community is very inclusive, so I've always felt part of it.

on there as well. And authors can hopefully find us through searching on Amazon for marketing advice."

Ricardo has a big presence at conferences. He speaks and socializes with the authors and is known affectionately in the author community as "Spanish Jesus." Does it feel different now that he's written a book himself?

"The indie author community is very inclusive, so I've always felt part of it. But it's true that one of the reasons I wrote the book is because I was being asked the question, "So what are you writing?" Which is the number one question you ask someone you don't know at a writing conference. And so I had to say, "No, I don't write." So I thought, I'm going to write a book, and I'm finally going to have a better answer to that question. And you know what? Since I've released a book, I think no one has asked me, what are you writing? I hope I meet someone at the next conference to ask this question."

IS THERE ANYTHING IN THE PIPELINE YOU WOULD LIKE US TO KNOW ABOUT?

According to Ricardo, Reedsy is working on redesigning their marketplace to provide an even better experience for people visiting it and to make it simpler for new authors to understand who they should hire.

"We're going to be adding features to make it collaborative so that you can write in real time with all the authors and you can share it with editors directly."

If you're looking for Ricardo out in the wild, he'll be at 20Books Madrid; SPF Live in London; The Indie Unconference in Matera, Italy; NINC; and 20Books Vegas. Online, he can be found at reedsy.com and on all the usual social media platforms. He's happy to receive emails at Ricardo@retail.com. ■

Elaine Bateman

Plotting a Book vs. a Screenplay

You've finished your novel, published it, received rave reviews, and sold lots of copies, and now you want something more for your story. You can see your characters on the big or little screen, living out the words you wrote and entertaining those who may not otherwise know of your book. You aren't sure where to begin, and you cannot afford a screenwriter, so you decide to initiate the transition from book to screen by creating your own screenplay. But writing a screenplay is much different than writing a book, and blindly jumping into this type of writing will leave you flailing in the forgotten pits of the movie and TV industries. Yet it can be done as many novelists have proven. The only sure way to give you a chance at success is by learning about writing screenplays.

Screenwriter John August notes a vital difference between the novel and the screenplay: "Novels are a final art form—you write a book and that's it … Screenplays, on the other hand, are one link in a long process leading to the final art form: a movie" (https://johnaugust.com/2007/novel-or-script). This basic distinction provides a lot more insight than one might first think. It states that your screenplay is not the final product and, therefore, is not written how a novel is. This becomes clearer when you plot your screenplay.

The plot of your screenplay or novel is the major events that occur. The story is the dramatic telling of those events. While plotting a screenplay and novel are similar in that regard, the screenplay plot resides within three acts while the novel is often told in five stages (exposition, rising action, climax, falling action, and resolution) but ultimately doesn't require a strict structure. The three acts of a screenplay are the setup, the confrontation, and the resolution. Within these acts, many parts of your story occur, but the structure of the screenplay is always the same.

The first act, the setup, introduces your hero and secondary characters while also revealing the inciting incident, which is the first plot point and occurs at the end of the act. This demonstrates the main conflict and drives the movie toward the next act. The second act includes raising the stakes of your conflict so as to heighten the need for resolution. This part of the screenplay also includes obstacles for your hero to overcome as well as the midpoint of the movie, which usually is a story twist followed by crisis or disaster. This leads to the height of the climax and right into Act III. The third act includes the descending action, resolution of the conflict (bad or good), and the end.

> The plot of your screenplay or novel is the major events that occur. The story is the dramatic telling of those events.

Once you have the structure down, you will usually follow that with a beat sheet, which "identifies the key emotional moments in a story, while the outline expands on those moments with specific scenes, settings, and details" (https://www.masterclass.com/articles/what-is-a-beat-in-screenwriting#4-types-of-story-beats). This Master-class article not only breaks down each section of a beat sheet but provides twelve steps for creating your own before writing the screenplay.

The three acts and beat sheets are vital to screenwriting; however, just as with novels, unless you read screenplays, it is extremely difficult to learn how to write and plot one. Author and screenwriter Solomon J. Powell highly recommends ScriptSlug (https://www.scriptslug.com) as a valuable resource. This tool assisted him in his own journey of transitioning from children's book author to screenwriter. He recommends reading the most current scripts. Although the older classic movie scripts offer excellent information, the guidelines on writing screenplays change often, and the newest scripts will reveal the latest formats.

But it's not always enough to just read the screenplays. Novelist and screenwriter Oz Mari Granlund advises you to read multiple scripts while you watch the movies. By doing this, you can see how the three acts and plot points are put into action. You can use the scripts while watching to identify the importance of plot structure in a movie. Then, watch movies without the script to find these elements on your own. This gives you excellent guidance in how to master the structure, and once you have a solid grip on it, you're ready to begin your screenplay. This is where the differences

between novels and screenplays can really confuse you if you're not prepared.

When reading screenplays, you will find little to no description. As novelists, we drench our work in description because we provide the entire visual for the reader. No movie or TV screen shows the reader what is happening. Unfortunately, that can translate into trying to write a screenplay because we want to show our vision for the final product. But writing too much detail into a screenplay can not only bog down your script but also encroaches on the director's role. Remembering the words of John August, the screenplay is only one step in the making of a movie or series. The screenwriter is simply the writer of the script. The director takes that script and uses their creative vision to bring the script to life on screen. So how much description should you use? Final Draft, a popular screenwriting software, states on its website that "each section of description should be contained to four lines or less" (http://finaldraft.com/ learn/write-better-de- scription-screen- play). This is why reading scripts of already- made movies is so

important. Those will show you acceptable levels of description and help you learn where your novelist brain needs to back off.

When writing a screenplay, remember the basic rule that one page generally equals one minute of screen time. This will help guide you in what goes on the page. If your first screenplay is three hundred pages, you'll instantly know this is approximately a five-hour movie, which won't work. Research the length of popular movies in your genre to assist you in knowing how many pages are needed. But keep in mind that just because *Hamlet* clocks in at just over four hours doesn't mean your script should, especially if you are a novice to screenwriting. A typical screenplay runs between 80 and 130 pages, and a long script from a first-time writer can be a red flag to studios and producers who sift through screenplays and dump approximately 95 percent of the ones on their desks.

When going back and reducing your script to an acceptable page number, ensure that you are not removing anything that will create plot holes. These can easily occur when you eliminate something vital to your three acts, plot points, or beat sheet. If you've ever watched a movie that seems to be missing something important to tie sections together, you'll understand the importance of not leaving plot holes in your final script. Scripts can be shortened by removing tropes, excessive dialogue that doesn't move your story forward, and fluffy adjectives. Just watch those plot holes because, as Granlund says, "Plot holes aren't cool."

While so much is involved in developing and writing a screenplay, you will be off to a great start of turning yourself from novelist to screenwriter and being successful in both worlds by following these guidelines and researching the craft. ■

Angie Martin

Build A *successful* International Writing Career

Eliminate the guesswork. Receive the essential, individual advice and practical support you need to launch, promote, and sell your German translations.

Join the Romancing Germany community and benefit from:

- STEP-BY-STEP INSTRUCTIONS
- CHECKLISTS & TEMPLATES
- MONTHLY INTERACTIVE Q&A SESSIONS
- SUPPORTIVE ONLINE COMMUNITY
- EXCLUSIVE RESOURCES & DISCOUNTS

SIGN UP NOW TO GET PERSONAL ACCESS TO THE PERSON BEHIND ROMANCING GERMANY, KRIS ALICE HOHLS, AND TAP INTO HER 20+ YEARS EXPERIENCE IN THE INDUSTRY.

"Working with Kris Alice has made my launch into Germany such a great success. Highly recommend signing up."
– USA Today bestselling author, Sasha Cottman

www.romancinggermany.com

3 ESSENTIAL ARCS FOR CRAFTING STRONG CHARACTERS AND SHAPING YOUR STORY

character death. A final goodbye. A heartfelt reunion. The end of a journey. It doesn't necessarily matter the specific plot points that elicit the emotion, nor is genre or artistic medium all that important. But scroll through recommendations on BookTok or consider the moments from a favorite series that have stuck with you the longest, and the phenomenon is plain to see. Almost inexplicably, readers enjoy reading books that make them cry.

It's not just tears, of course. Any emotions that can echo from somewhere on the page out to your readers in the real world are powerful. Aristotle called the concept "the paradox of tragedy." According to him—and the philosophers and storytellers who've pondered the idea since—audiences like experiencing emotions, be they happy, sad, or something in between.

But what's the secret to writing them?

Characters. More specifically, character arcs. A character's inner transformation over the course of a story has the potential to shape the plot and prove its significance, according to Kristen Kieffer's writing craft blog, Well-Storied (https://www.well-storied.com). Write it well, and that character will provide emotional weight for readers over the course of your story—maybe even enough for them to feel those emotions themselves.

"In my view, character arc is the 'demonstration' of a story's theme as executed through the plot," writes novelist and writing teacher K.M. Weiland. "Character arc ties it all together, providing both forward movement in the external plot and meaning through the theme." In her book *Creating Character Arcs: The Masterful Author's Guide to Uniting Story Structure*, Weiland details the three types of character arcs. But not every protagonist will follow the same arc, and deciding which arcs fit your characters involves understanding not just the events they face but also how they will ultimately be shaped by them.

> "In my view, character arc is the 'demonstration' of a story's theme as executed through the plot." —K.M. Weiland

1. POSITIVE ARC: THE HEROIC RISE

Example: Neo, *The Matrix*

Arguably the easiest to recognize and most well-known, a positive arc traces a character's journey in overcoming a dark outlook on life or an internal fear to come to a more positive belief. In Weiland's book, she addresses these initial and changed outlooks as "the lie" and "the truth," respectively. Characters with positive arcs start out believing a lie about themselves or the world around them but, through the course of the story, are able to overcome that lie and discover a truth that is ultimately freeing.

Positive arcs are easy to spot among protagonists in today's stories, especially for characters who seek to grow into a new role in society or who face adversity over the course of a novel and rise above it. They might be easiest to spot in coming-of-age novels or fantasy epics that feature a "chosen one" trope. But not every positive arc has to be wielded by a main character—side characters and even antagonists can experience the same moral growth as long as they end the story with a more positive outlook than they had when it began.

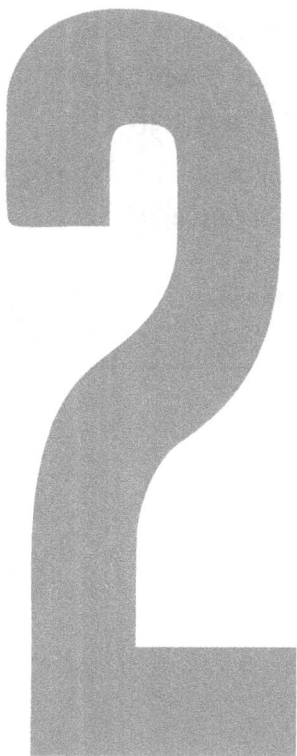

2. NEGATIVE ARC: THE DOWNWARD SPIRAL

Example: Anakin Skywalker, *Star Wars: Episode III—Revenge of the Sith*

Just as some characters rise, so do other characters fall. That's the case with characters with negative arcs, who often start a novel believing a lie about themselves or the world, similar to those with positive arcs. However, rather than settling on a more positive belief, these characters end their arc with the realization of a more negative truth—or sometimes a separate, even worse lie, according to <u>the Writing Cooperative</u> (<u>https://writingcooperative.com</u>). This arc is often seen with antagonists, but that's not always the case.

In the same way that antagonists can follow positive arcs, many famous protagonists become the "tragic heroes" who follow negative arcs. The terms "protagonist" and "antagonist" are morally neutral, writes Weiland, meaning characters aren't automatically required to follow a certain character arc simply because of the role they play in a story. "We often find protagonists undergoing 'negative' arcs leading either to disillusionment or even moral degradation while antagonists can sometimes be the most 'positive' or 'moral' characters in the story."

In her book, Weiland defined negative arcs further by creating subcategories such as "disillusionment" and "corruption." Initially, she believed there were simply more ways of "doing things wrong," she writes. However, now, she prefers to approach all arcs as part of a spectrum. "Ultimately, the characterizations here are just describing the various ways people interact with the transition from an outdated perspective to a new and more functional perspective." Even characters with morally gray outlooks can have net positive or net negative arcs as long as their beliefs change slightly for the better or for the worse, respectively.

But what about characters whose viewpoints don't change?

3. FLAT ARC: THE TRIED AND TRUE

Example: Sherlock Holmes

Not every character changes viewpoints over the course of a story, but that doesn't necessarily mean they exist without an arc. Characters whose beliefs are tested but ultimately do not waver are said to have flat arcs, and though their outlooks don't change by the resolution of their arcs, they're far from static, according to iWriterly (https://iwriterly.com).

The key difference is doubt, Weiland writes. On her writing blog, Helping Writers Become Authors, she explains that characters with flat arcs still grapple with a lie and a truth. These characters already possess the truth, but as the story goes on, they must begin to doubt their truth in favor of the lie that others around them believe. By the end of the story, however, they should be able to return to their initial truth, more resolved and steadfast than before.

The flat arc is especially common in episodic stories, such as those in Cozy Mystery or Thriller genres. It's also frequently seen among established superheroes—though a superhero's origin story can sometimes involve a positive arc instead. In fact, when it comes to characters in a series, Weiland suggests multiple ways of considering their arcs: as individual arcs to be contained within each book, as large overarching arcs to develop over the course of an entire series, or, she writes on her blog, as a combination of the two. Creating multiple small arcs to be contained within a larger arc over the course of a series, she writes, has the potential to add even more depth and complexity to your character—and to make your story even more memorable for your readers.

Three arc types might feel constricting, and some writing guides include additional arcs, such as the transformation arc, for stories in which authors struggle to assign strictly positive, negative, or flat arcs to their characters. But Weiland finds that those additional arc classifications are often variations on the main three, which are broadly defined on purpose. "There are endless varieties on a theme, and exceptions to every rule," she writes. "I do find that most stories fit into one of those categories, and they usually resonate most strongly when they align the character's transformation properly to the story's structure."

Ultimately, finding your characters' arcs might still take some time. But the best way to understand and internalize the arc structures, Weiland writes, "is to study them in your favorite books and movies." Perfecting your characters' arcs can't guarantee a bestseller—in this industry, nothing is ever quite that definitive. But paying as much attention to each character's inner journey as you do to their physical odyssey could be just the detail that moves your story from good to worthy of your readers' real-world emotions. ■

Nicole Schroeder

Get documents done anywhere

Now available for your Android & iOS mobile device

Dragon® Anywhere professional-grade mobile dictation makes it easy to create documents of any length, edit, format and share them directly from your mobile device-whether visiting clients, a job site, or your local coffee shop.

- ✅ Continuous dictation and no word limits
- ✅ 99% accurate with powerful voice editing and formatting
- ✅ Access customized words and auto-text across all devices
- ✅ Share documents by email, Dropbox, Evernote and more

Select a flexible pricing plan   **Subscribe now** ▾   *Credit Card Required. After your 7 day free trial, the monthly subscription begins at $15 per month. Cancel at anytime.*

WriteLink.To/Dragon

ATTICUS

A WRITER'S GOLDILOCKS SOLUTION FOR WRITING, EDITING, AND FORMATTING

A lot of buzz surrounds the brand-new software Atticus, the brainchild of Dave Chesson, the founder of <u>Kindlepreneur</u>.

Atticus has been described as the love child between the well-established programs Vellum and Scrivener. Early access was by invite only, but since the beginning of November, the app is available for purchase at <u>https://atticus.io</u>.

The software not only allows you to write your novel within an intuitive interface but also makes it easy to format and export your work, ready to upload to the various retail sites.

Atticus has only recently come out of the beta stage. This fully functioning software has some more features coming down the pipeline, including global find and replace, word trackers, and integration with popular tools like Grammarly and ProWritingAid.

The app allows the user to write their draft directly into the software and automatically saves and backs it up to the cloud. Once the writer is happy with their words, they can style the text in a number of ways.

You can insert front and back matter, collate your books into series, and save templates to make formatting easier for subsequent works.

WHAT MAKES ATTICUS DIFFERENT FROM ITS COMPETITORS?

Vellum

Atticus is available both as an app and as an online software. You can write offline or on your phone, and your work will be synchronized to the cloud server.

The app can be downloaded on iOS, Windows, smartphones, and on Chromebooks. And herein lies the major difference to the aforementioned Vellum.

Vellum's software is only available for the Mac. If you're on a PC, you need to use other programs that often require a steep learning curve. Alternatively, you can outsource the formatting to contractors, which quickly adds up from book to book. You also have to go back and renegotiate every time you need to update your back matter, re-edit, or even just correct typos.

Many writers buy MacBooks just to run Vellum because it makes converting your Word document into an e-book or paperback a breeze. However, Atticus does the exact same thing on multiple platforms.

When it comes to exporting, Atticus may prove just as powerful as Vellum. Creating an e-book or paperback is as easy as clicking a button from several locations within the app.

Scrivener and Google Docs

Scrivener is the preferred software for many writers. Those who like a simpler interface use Google Docs or Word. Atticus is not quite as feature-laden as Scrivener, but it offers more capabilities than a Word document.

Scrivener has more functions than Atticus in terms of organizing research, tagging, and integrating editing software like ProWritingAid.

Exporting your finished document can be particularly irksome in Scrivener. It takes time to learn how to use the settings, and more time to test the exports with the various distributors. What KDP accepts as a final EPUB could differ from Draft2Digital, for example. Atticus allows for exporting your work as a publishing-ready EPUB or PDF as well as a DOCX version for backup and editing.

A CLOSER LOOK AT ATTICUS

Atticus occupies the space between a lot and not enough when it comes to functionality and versatility.

The interface is intuitive and easy to use with two main buttons, writing and formatting.

Pro Tip: Watch the tutorials at this link: https://atticus.io/tutorials. They are exceptionally useful to quickly answer any questions you might have.

The writing screen shows front matter, back matter, and body chapters listed on the left, which you can move around as needed. You can set a counter to show you a word count per document, chapter, or for a selection.

Pro Tip: You can easily save front and back matter elements like the copyright page or your back catalog listings as templates. That way, you can insert them in any future books so they don't have to be recreated.

You can set a timer for whatever duration you require. An added break option allows for a Pomodoro interval. Other options include setting a book goal, which keeps track of word count toward that goal, and a writing habit tracker.

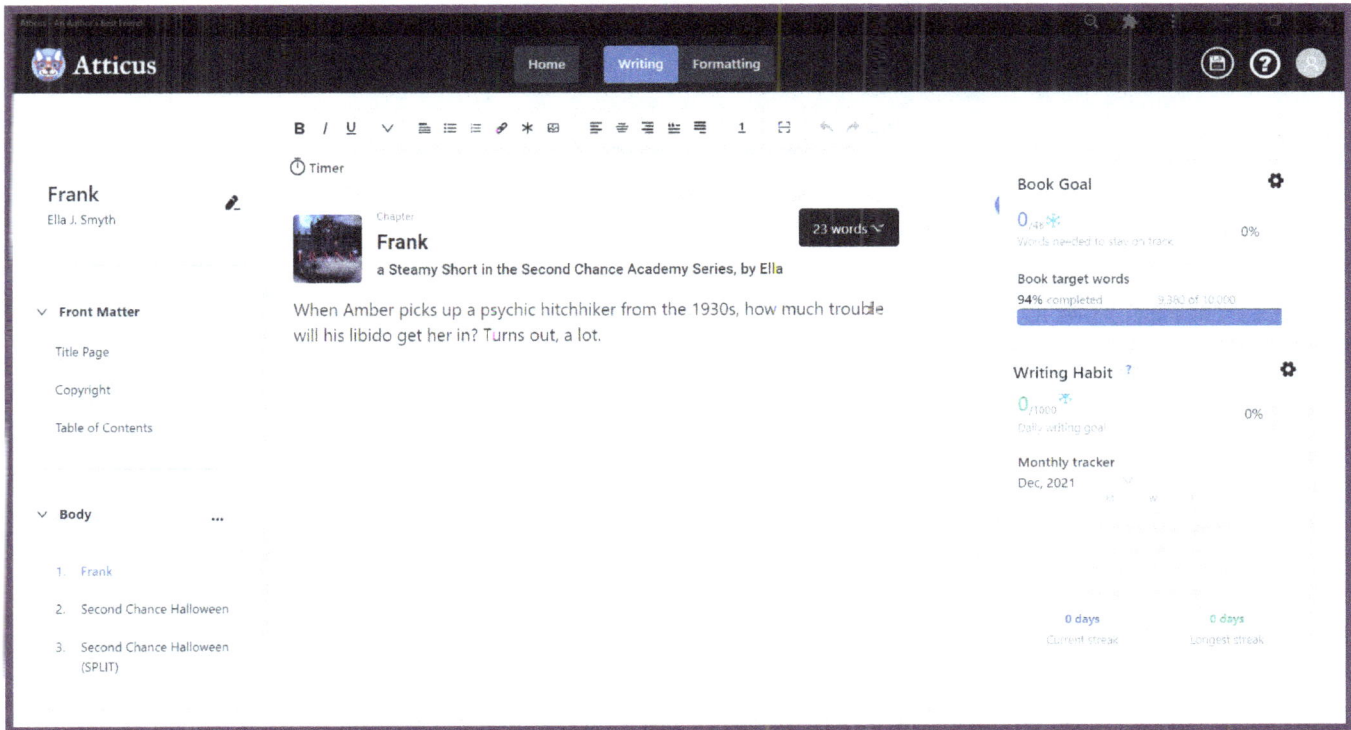

During the beta stage, users complained about a lack of available text-formatting styles. Atticus now offers seventeen different templates. More importantly, you can also create a custom template with the font and even background image of your choice.

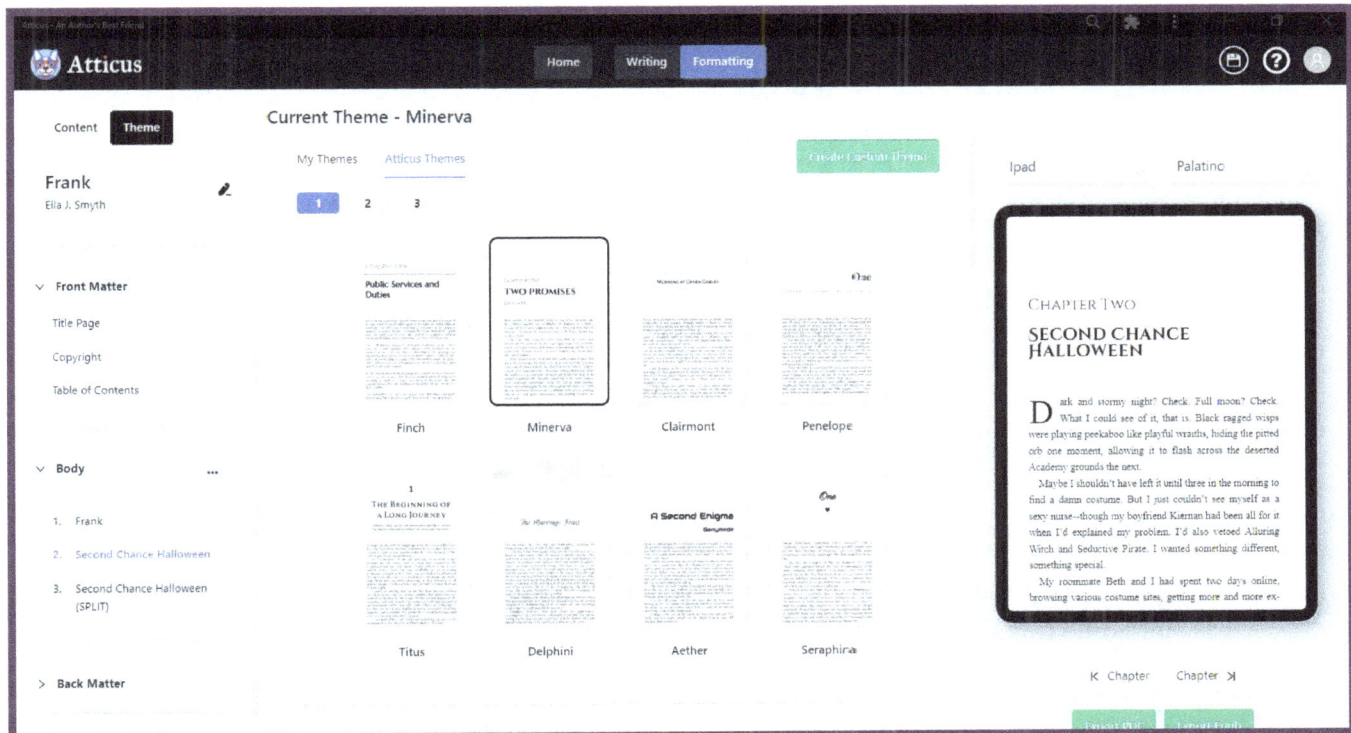

Atticus also offers thirty-six ornamental page breaks with the option to import your own custom image. You can choose from fifteen different fonts for paperbacks, all popular trim plus custom sizes, and large print options. Formats supported by KDP and IngramSpark are clearly indicated.

The paperback settings include a choice of eight headers and footers. As you would expect, drop cap and paragraph indentation are options for the beginning of each chapter.

A preview panel on the right allows for instantaneous feedback on how your work will appear not only on the Kindle but also on Nook, Android, and Kobo devices.

Exporting the finished book into both PDF and EPUB takes just one click. Creating paperbacks is just as simple. Select the size and format before exporting the book, ready to upload to the retail website of your choice.

WHAT ELSE DOES ATTICUS OFFER?

Atticus allows the user to split chapters and integrate them into the running order without renumbering them individually.

You can import your work in progress from various formats: RTF, DOCX, EPUB, and MOBI. However, DOCX is the preferred option though it might take a little trial and error to seamlessly move existing documents into Atticus. For example, it works best to strip out the table of contents since Atticus creates its own.

Are you our next Featured Author?

Tell us your story!

writelink.to/featured

Pro Tip: When importing a word document, keep in mind that Atticus automatically formats Heading One and 20-point font (or larger) as chapter titles and Heading Two and 18-point font as subheadings. It also recognizes page breaks or three consecutive empty lines as new chapters.

You can even add full-bleed images, which aren't cut off at the margins. Atticus also supports footnotes and endnotes.

WHAT'S NEXT FOR ATTICUS?

Dave Chesson's team confirmed that a ProWritingAid integration is in the works. So is gamification of word count goals and dark mode.

One new feature will be a Word-style editing tool that allows your editor and beta readers to work directly with your document while you retain control over the changes. Chesson also plans to make a plotting tool available in the future to help with outlining, character development, and world building.

PROMISING, BUT NOT YET PERFECT

Atticus will roll out new features in the coming months, and all future upgrades are included in the one-off payment.

The app, at the time of writing, boasts a price tag of $149 for a lifetime license with unlimited project creation and exports of both e-books and paperbacks. Vellum, in comparison, charges $249 for their combined option.

If you're still on the fence, the software offers a thirty-day money-back guarantee.

Over to you: Do you already use Atticus? What do you think? Do you have any tips for your fellow authors? Let us know via email to feedback@ indieauthormagazine.com. ∎

Marion Hermannsen

Tech Tools

Courtesy of IndieAuthorTools.com
Got a tool you love and want to share with us?
Submit a tool at IndieAuthorTools.com

Story Structure Database

The Story Structure Database is a free archive of movies and books, recording their major plot points. This is a valuable resource when you have story structure questions. Just search the database, on K.M. Weiland's website, to find answers and examples.
https://www.helpingwritersbecomeauthors.com/story-structures/

Kindlepreneur

Wonder how to make your book description eye-catching? Check out the Kindlepreneur Book Description Generator. This free tool helps you easily generate the HTML code you need for your book description for websites such as Amazon, Barnes & Noble, and Rakuten. It was designed to help you build good-looking book descriptions, which can help you sell more books.
https://kindlepreneur.com/amazon-book-description-generator/

Plottr

Plottr is a visual book outlining software that helps you outline your novel and organize your ideas. If you don't want to plot your story from scratch, you can use any of the 14 templates that are included. Based on proven storytelling structures, the templates range from The Hero's Journey to Romancing the Beat. Plottr automatically generates an outline based on the content of your visual timelines. You can export your work to Word and Scrivener. Annual or lifetime subscriptions, based on number of devices, are available.
https://plottr.com/

---

freedom

Focus on what matters by controlling distractions with the Freedom app. Social media, videos, shopping places, games ... they're scientifically engineered to keep you visiting again and again. The cost to your productivity and general well-being can be astounding. Freedom puts you back in control. Free trial available.
https://freedom.to

Linkjoy

Instagram bios only allow one link, so you'd better make it count if you want to actually convert the followers enjoying your free content.
Looking for a way to increase traffic to your site and retarget one-time visitors by maximizing your bio link? Say hello to Linkjoy, an alternative to linktree.
appsumo.8odi.net/rnbdrR

The ABCs of Publishing Picture Books

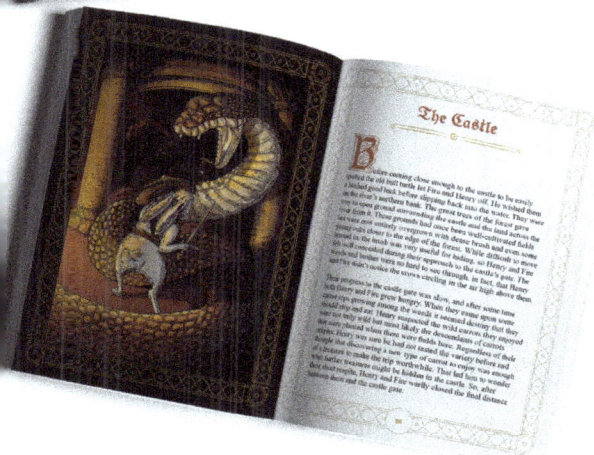

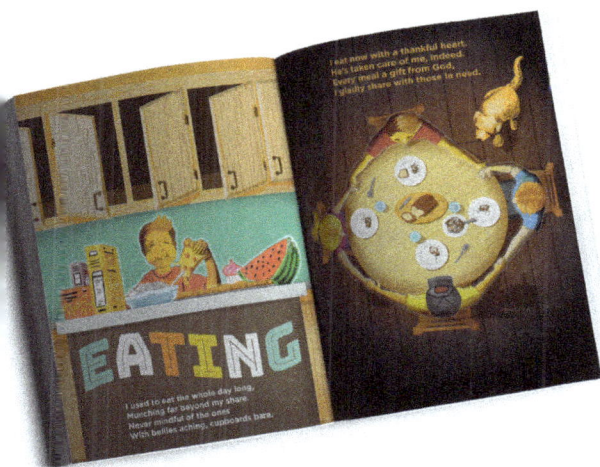

They say a picture is worth a thousand words—but if that's the case, the exchange rate into dollars must be equally impressive. After all, picture books in the US children's book market are worth $2.6 billion, according to IBISWorld (https://ibisworld.com/industry-statistics/market-size/childrens-book-publishing-united-states).

Picture books are written and published for children ages three to eight. Typically, parents read to their children on the younger side of that range, and as the child's independent reading skills develop, they will read the books themselves. From nine years on, children generally prefer chapter books with the length increasing with age and reading level. This important demographic is worthy of your consideration, but the mechanics of production are much the same as a novel or other book for an adult with some unique aspects.

YOUR CHOICES

Trim size

This is the size of your book typically shown as width x height, e.g., 8x10 inches. Kindle Direct Publishing (KDP), IngramSpark, and Barnes &

Noble produce full color POD books suitable for children's books, and their distribution is the same as for all other self-published books. KDP's minimum page count for hardcovers is seventy-six, which is over double the typical length of a picture book. Not all trim sizes are available on all platforms, so make sure that your chosen trim size is available everywhere you wish to distribute.

If you're unsure what sizes are appropriate for your book, visit your local library and bring a tape measure. Many online platforms may list the trim size as well. While you're doing your research, you can also take note of what you see and like related to the following choices. Traditionally published books have a wider range of trim sizes than POD, but you're still likely to find a greater variety within indie published titles than on the typical novel shelf. Your investigations can also tell you if portrait (height is greater than width), landscape (width is greater than height), or square (width and height are equal) formats are more common or closer to what you prefer.

Illustrations

You'll want to determine the style of illustrations and the type that you want for your book. Are they sharp and solid? Are they soft and flowing? Vibrant colors or muted? Black and white or full color? Artists have their own style, so you'll want to find and work with an illustrator that suits your style and book.

To find an illustrator, you can join children's author and illustrator groups on Facebook or look on art sites for an artist with a style you like. Most illustrators are acknowledged on the cover or within a book, so you can also glance through children's books and contact an artist directly if you like their work. Most illustrators who work with traditional publishing houses have an agent, so you may need to dig deeper to find the agent's contact information. Some authors work with emerging artists in their local community. If you work with an artist who doesn't typically illustrate books, you'll probably need to work more closely with them to help them understand margins and bleeds as well as the way the text may interact with their artwork.

Bleed is an extra border outside the trim size of the page so that the full color of the illustration that goes to the edge of the page never has a white border or blank page unless the printing process has gone seriously awry.

Full page spread above

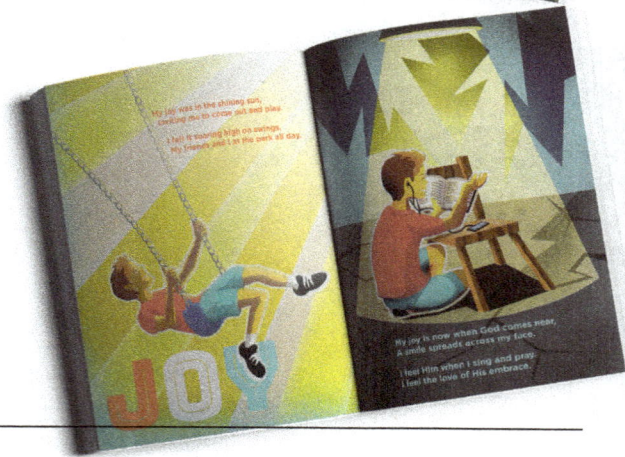

Full pages above and below

Vignettes above and below

What we're calling the type of image includes vignette, full-page, and full-spread images. Full-page and full-spread images will need to account for page bleed while vignettes should fit on the page without encroaching on the edges. For POD purposes, the size of the illustration doesn't affect the cost. Any color on any page makes the entire book in color, so your cost will not be affected by those variances.

The size and complexity of the illustration will probably affect the cost of the illustrations themselves though, so work with your illustrator to come up with a package that will best suit your book. You can use a variety of illustrations throughout the entire book.

Remember that the illustrations are as important as your words. Your illustrator is your partner and ally—not your adversary—throughout this process. This should be a win-win-win process for all involved: for you, for the illustrator, and for the children who will read and love your book.

PUTTING IT TOGETHER

Once you have your illustrations and your manuscript edited, it's time to format your book. POD platforms require a single PDF file for the interior of your book as pages and with the appropriate bleed if needed. You'll also want to tick the appropriate box for with bleed or without when uploading your files for best results.

Formatting a children's book can be done in InDesign, a robust publishing program part of the Adobe Creative Cloud suite, though you can also pay $20.99 per month for InDesign alone. The program has a fairly steep learning curve, although this would be lower for a picture book than for a more complex document. If that seems too pricey, Affinity Publisher is an InDesign alternative available for a onetime fee of $59.12 instead of as a subscription.

Other children's book authors report using alternatives such as Canva, Google Slides, or PowerPoint. As long as you can export your interior as a single PDF in your trim size, you should be fine.

You'll need to have your illustrations created at sufficient size so that your formatted book will

be 300 dots per inch for high-quality printing. To calculate this, multiply your trim size—plus bleed if needed—by 300. A trim size of 8x10 inches without bleed would be 2400x3000 pixels.

The interior file specs will be the same for both paperback and hardcover and also for KDP and IngramSpark. Barnes & Noble has larger margin requirements, but their bleed requirements are the same as the other two distributors.

COVER

Cover files are unique to the individual platforms. There will be some similarities between these, so a complete redesign should not be required. Hardcover books require larger dimensions than paperbacks as the design needs to wrap around the board and onto the inside of the cover. If you think you may want to do hardcover at some point, it's good practice to create for that file size, or have your illustrator create large enough artwork so you have that option when you're ready for it. It's easier to crop something shorter than to create additional length.

When commissioning your illustrations, consider if you will need a separate design for the cover or if you will reuse one from the interior. If you want the image to extend throughout the entire cover, then you'll want to confirm the size needed on the platform of your choice. Allow for a bit of extra room so that you don't risk coming up short.

UPLOAD AND SET PRICES

There's no question that POD is a more expensive option than an off-set print run. Color makes this even more apparent. Recently, IngramSpark has adjusted their prices, so consider using the royalty calculators on each site you use to choose a price that will work for all.

And now you know how to create your own POD picture book and get your piece of that $2.6 billion market. As with many elements of the indie

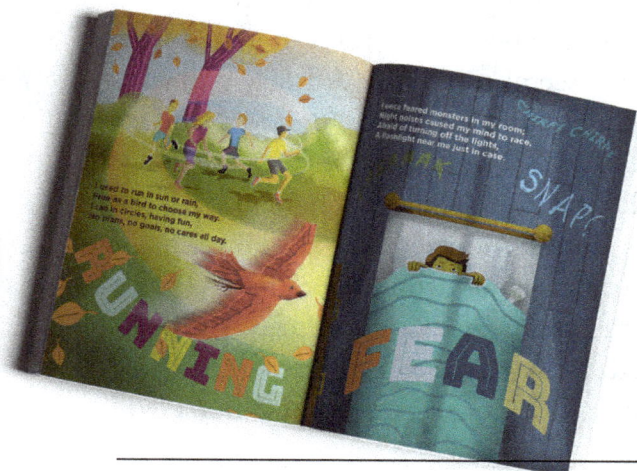

publishing industry, there are a lot of moving pieces, but if you take them step-by-step, you'll soon be hitting the publish button and celebrating a job well done.

Note: Picture books are board books for babies, books on very thick paper or boards. At the time of this writing, we were unable to discover any print-on-demand options for board books. Your options are a large print run and then shipping them yourself or with places such as Fulfilled by Amazon. If you know of a POD board book printer we missed, please let us know at feedback@indieauthormagazine.com! ■

Alice Briggs

YOU MAY ALSO LIKE:

"Hardbacks Made Easy" in February 2022's issue

"Cover Your Backside: Creating A Full Wrap For Print Without Tears" in October 2021's issue for a more thorough discussion of creating the cover for your POD book in both paperback and hardcover

Self-Publishing a Children's Book: ALLi's Guide to Kidlit Publishing for Authors (Publishing Guides for Indie Authors Book 7)

BOOKS FEATURED:

The Acorn and the Oak
  Author: Rhonda Accardo
  Illustrator: Jessica Waterstradt
The Adventures of Henry the Rabbit King: The Green Valley
  Author: Jesse Abbott
  Illustrator: Phillip Ortiz
The Boy in Two Places
  Author: Luke Fredenberg
  Illustrator: Phillip Ortiz
The New Earth: You're Gonna Love It
  by Kathi DeCanio
  Illustrator: Phillip Ortiz

Podcasts We Love

Author Matty Dalrymple delves into how we can improve our writing skills and navigate a career in self-publishing on The Indy Author Podcast. Dalrymple, who is lauded for her interview technique, launches new episodes of the show weekly. In addition, you can learn about the tools and resources that have been indispensable to her as an author at theindyauthor.com.

https://www.theindyauthor.com/podcast.html

For "all things story" check out Narrative First. The show is no longer active, but 66 episodes "aimed at providing the secrets to great storytelling" are archived. The mostly evergreen content covers "screenplays to novels to deep theoretical story structure."

https://podcasts.apple.com/us/podcast/narrative-first-where-story-is-always-king/id1131426809

Dan Simpson looks "inside the daily diary of a writer, to peek at the secrets of their success" on his award-winning Writer's Routine show. He interviews authors, from aspiring to famous, for tips, tricks, and inspiration that could help us on our indie author journey. The weekly podcast airs on Fridays.

https://podcasts.apple.com/us/podcast/writers-routine/id1273996998

CRIMINAL JUSTICE

In the criminal justice system, the people are represented by two separate yet equally important groups: the police, who investigate crime; and the district attorneys, who prosecute the offenders. These are their stories. —*Law & Order*.

In a gamut of literary genres including Mystery, Police Procedural, Legal Thriller, and Prison Literature, the readers are represented by authors, whose understanding of the details can provide verisimilitude, spotlight forensic and procedural advancements, and engage in the ongoing debate over social justice reforms. These can be your stories.

A potential source of conflict arises when the evidence tells a story that contradicts the investigators' theory of the case.

> In a fantasy setting, the limits of magics should shape an investigation as much as the limits of technology.

FORENSIC SCIENCE

Crime scene investigators scrutinize evidence in a slow and methodical process. Fictional accounts tend to highlight only the most shocking revelations. While you can and should compress time as needed to maintain the pacing of a story, a careless rush can minimize the painstaking care that goes into processing evidence while preventing avoidable contamination of a crime scene.

To be useful in an investigation and subsequent prosecution, the preservation of evidence requires a meticulously documented chain of custody. And while it's impressive for an investigator to recognize a scrap of fabric on sight as being of 2017 vintage, used by only one shirt manufacturer, and sold at five specific stores in the city, at least one person should double-check such claims. "Jones is always right about this kind of thing" is a poor justification for committing department resources to tracking down a lead.

A potential source of conflict arises when the evidence tells a story that contradicts the investigators' theory of the case. What happens next can pivot the story in an entirely new direction. In the end, analysis in the lab may provide the building blocks for a theory of when, where, and how a crime may have taken place, but the why of the case, the motive in the perpetrator's mind, can never be proven by scientific analysis alone.

TECHNOLOGY IS EVERYWHERE

DNA analysis has opened up new lines of investigation that previously weren't available or as easily presented to a jury. Networks and databases allow better cross-jurisdiction collaboration to more easily and quickly sort through more information with more expertise. Cameras are in use at an ever-widening range of retail establishments, above busy intersections, and in residential doorbells. Mobile phones and smart watches are being used to reconstruct a suspect's communication, movement, and even heart rate while a crime was being committed. Social media and search histories can help reconstruct a suspect's state of mind for weeks or months leading up to a crime.

If a story is set in a specific time and place, the state of technology will matter. Projecting more advanced technology into a historical story is as common as failing to account for an advance available to investigators in contemporary or near-future settings. In a fantasy setting, the limits of magics should shape an investigation as much as the limits of technology.

> Some of the most powerful details in stories about the criminal justice system spotlight its flaws.

COURTROOM DRAMA

Trial scenes can inject high-stakes drama into a story. But if your trial takes place in a realistic setting and isn't intended as parody, you should familiarize yourself with the rules and practices of jury selection, arraignment, trial, plea agreements, and the admissibility or exclusion of evidence.

In a more realistic courtroom, the presiding judge controls proceedings, and theatrics are discouraged in most phases of the trial with summation statements being a possible exception. A lawyer must obtain the judge's permission to approach a witness during questioning, and only then for good reason, such as to show them a piece of evidence.

Lawyers aren't allowed to address the jury while questioning a witness, and an objection must be addressed on the record before further questions are allowed. Witnesses rarely incriminate themselves on the stand.

CRIMINAL JUSTICE REFORM

Some of the most powerful details in stories about the criminal justice system spotlight its flaws. Characters may struggle with issues of systemic bias, social injustice, substance abuse, economic inequality, government surveillance, and more. The incidents and attitudes depicted may invite an examination of our society, our history, and aspects of human nature itself.

You may be tempted to insert your own opinions into the minds and mouths of your characters. If you choose this path, be mindful, interrogate your own blind spots and biases, and as they say in the squad room, be careful out there.

Greg Fishbone

LIVING the ROMANTASY

Romantic Fantasy (AKA Romantasy) is a subgenre of Fantasy that pairs a strong romantic subplot with a Fantasy main plot. The focus can skew toward the Fantasy plot with a significant minority of romantic elements, or it can balance fairly evenly between the two.

Romantasy is often confused with its sister genre, Fantasy Romance. While the Venn diagram of their readership does overlap, distinct expectations mean readers of one may not choose to read the other. If you like both, you're in luck: A quick look at the bestseller lists and Amazon charts shows the likes of Sarah J. Maas, Raven Kennedy, and Laura Thalassa flying high, proving that both genres sell for traditional publishers and indie authors alike.

ROMANTIC FANTASY AND FANTASY ROMANCE: WHAT'S THE DIFFERENCE?

Both genres tend to be written for women readers and feature romantic relationships, which can be heterosexual, LGBT+,

GENRE TROPES IN ROMANTIC FANTASY

or polyamorous (as foregrounded by reverse harem's success in recent years). They run the gamut in terms of heat level, from no hint of sexual desire even in characters' thoughts all the way to explicit sex scenes with four-letter anatomical terms. Whichever you choose, as with any Romance, it's advisable to signal the heat level to readers through marketing material, including covers and blurbs.

Where Romantic Fantasy is a subgenre of Fantasy, Fantasy Romance is a subgenre of Romance (some readers shelve it as "Fanrom"). As such, books in that subgenre obey the rules of Romance (e.g., ending with an HEA or HFN), broadly follow the Romance structure outlined in Gwen Hayes' *Romancing the Beat*, and tend to have a single or dual point of view. Each book in a series generally follows a different couple. They are romances—they just happen to take place in a Fantasy setting. An example is Grace Draven's *Radiance*.

Romantic Fantasy books, on the other hand, follow Fantasy rules and expectations (some readers shelve these as "Romfan"). They tend to be longer (books longer than one hundred thousand words are common, and those beyond two hundred thousand words are still within normal parameters though fifty-thousand-word novels also exist within series) and will feature fantastical elements, such as magic, fantasy creatures, and worlds that, while influenced by the history of our own, are *not quite* the same.

They may or may not follow Romance rules; for example, the heroine might have multiple partners, as seen in *A Court of Thorns and Roses* when the central character moves from one love interest to another through the course of the series. An HEA/HFN is not guaranteed in Romantic Fantasy books; however, readers may still be disappointed if your epic love story doesn't end happily.

Books in a series tend to follow the same central characters as they face various trials and tribulations and may feature single, dual, or multiple points of view. Raven Kennedy's *The Plated Prisoner* series, beginning with *Gild*, is a recent example.

When trying to remember which is which, it's helpful to keep in mind the second word is the noun (Romantic *Fantasy* or Fantasy *Romance*) or its core genre while the first word is the adjective that tells you what kind of Fantasy or Romance.

KEY FEATURES OF ROMANTIC FANTASY

While most Fantasy tropes can find a home in Romantic Fantasy, readers have specifically come to expect some key elements from this genre.

These stories are at their core Fantasy adventures. That could take the form of finding the MacGuffin, saving the world from the evil overlord, or even becoming the evil overlord in a more villainous take on the genre. (Indeed, villain Romance, a romantic trope, translates well into the genre.)

That being said, readers do expect the romance to be significant and take up screen time: The brief mentions of romance in *The Lord of the Rings*, for example, don't qualify it as Romantic Fantasy and would disappoint the genre's readers.

Ultimately, we come to Romantic Fantasy for stories that combine adventure and romance and allow us to escape the mundane world for as long as it takes to turn a few (or several) hundred pages.

COMMON TROPES IN ROMANTIC FANTASY

A female lens: The readership is largely made up of women: they want to read narratives that foreground women and their stories. Where the heroine loves a hero, he needs to be likable (and loveable) to the women reading.

The meet cute: Romantic Fantasy readers expect this Romance staple—the moment the protagonist meets their love interest. As with Romance, the couple may already know each other (as in the case of friends to lovers), but they will still have a key moment that's the first time they share space on the page, which will form the foundation for their relationship in the reader's mind.

Strong heroine who saves the day: Most commonly books by women for women, these include fewer damsels in distress and plenty of dames doing the saving. Often, the love interests rescue each other at different points throughout a series.

Enemies to lovers: This bestselling Romance trope is just as popular in Romantic Fantasy with plenty of scope for inter-species prejudices and love across (literal) battle lines.

Friendship and found family: With the marriage of Romance and Fantasy, relationships are a key focus of this genre, and that goes for the platonic kind too. Even the hero who begins as the cool, aloof loner must eventually become part of a collective even if that's only through their partner.

Elemental magic: Who wouldn't want to be able to hurl fireballs or lightning bolts? Readers love characters who can do that too.

Fairytale retellings: A significant portion of Romantic Fantasy stories are retellings of fairy tales. This can range from a novel that closely follows the traditional *Beauty and the Beast* story to a looser reimagining with a hero who is cursed and a heroine whose love can save him as seen in the first book of Sarah J. Maas's *A Court of Thorns and Roses*. ■

Clare Sager

WRITING WITH

Chronic illness pervades the population, including that of writers. According to the CDC, six in ten adults suffer from a chronic illness while four in ten suffer from at least two chronic illnesses (https://cdc.gov/chronicdisease/tools/infographics.htm). These staggering statistics apply to writers as well, creating another challenge for those affected in an already difficult and complex industry.

Writing with chronic illness looks much different than writing without—and so does self-care. We often think of self-care as what we see prevalent in commercials or on the internet: spa days, vacations, etc. While these are nice, self-care for the chronically ill takes on a much simpler plan. It is more about taking your medications, seeing your doctor, seeking help if depression sinks in, staying comfortable, opening a window to let it sun and fresh air, and maybe taking a bubble bath if and when you can. Your health is your first priority; your occupation as a writer should always come second.

Before you can write, you should first evaluate your limitations due to your chronic illness. Finding a comfortable area to write in or adapting your writing area to accommodate your condition is important to staying healthy. If you try to write in chronic pain, for instance, you're more likely to focus on the illness rather than on writing. In addition, you might need to change your writing schedule. For example, you may only be able to write in fifteen-minute intervals, and that's okay. There is no rule that you must sit for hours on end to be a writer.

Ensuring your self-care routine is set and creating an ideal writing space is only part of the challenge. A support system is a must, and this can be found in family, friends, and other writers. Align with others in the industry who also suffer from chronic illness. They can assist you in so many ways, including providing forums to discuss your illness, accessing tips on how to make writing easier, and offering a place to lift yourself back up if you start to spiral. Places like Facebook have tons of groups dedicated to chronic illness, where you can find other writers in the same spot as you.

CHRONIC ILLNESS

No matter how you approach chronic illness as a writer, always remember to apply self-care first and have that strong support system. By taking the time to manage your chronic illness and prioritize what your body needs, you'll find you gain more time to focus on that thing we all love: writing. ■

Angie Martin

YOU GO FASTER WHEN YOU GO SLOWER

THE POWER OF SLOW

The indie author life can easily swamp authors with opportunity. The writing life can turn into a weary slog that never seems to bring success any closer. What if there was another way to supercharge your career?

REST

Rest is the key to making connections, gaining insights, and creating inspired work.

After an extended pilgrimage hike, Joanna Penn was initially frustrated that she didn't get any massive insight: "A few weeks later, I ended up going into almost a flow state, and I wrote two books in about four weeks (*Your Author Business Plan* and *Artificial Intelligence, Blockchain and Virtual Worlds*) and launched them, and I had some of the most insightful thinking I've had in a long time."

REDUCE

Can you narrow down your writing and publishing goals to one or two?

When author Shawn Inman was asked how he got faster at the publishing biz, he said, "I stopped lying to myself". He decided to simplify his process.

"Stop lying to yourself" is a powerful strategy for cutting "extra" goals out of your life. A life with fewer goals is also mentally more comfortable and leaves time for friends and family.

TEST AND TRUST

The surprising truth about creativity—both for manuscripts and marketing—is that going slower makes you go faster. Give yourself credit. You are gaining insights and information that you can't learn any other way. Don't lose this advantage.

"The only way to learn what works for you, and what doesn't, is to try things. The more you experiment, the harder you work, and the more you improve your craft, the shorter the Long Slow Slog will be. It'll still be long, mind you. If you practice business as well as your creative attitude, The Slog will prove your art could be a full-time career, or not," according to Michael W. Lucas in the book *Cash Flow for Creators*.

What if you tested the simplest possible plotting or drafting process built on trusting yourself? Think how much more time you'd have to work (and play!) if your creativity weren't hampered by fear or doubts.

REST, REDUCE, TEST, AND TRUST.

Next month, we'll cover ways to identify your essential work. You can do this. You go faster when you go slower.

PODCASTS

"Mind Management, Not Time Management With David Kadavy" (April 26, 2021) https://thecreativepenn.com/2021/04/26/mind-management-not-time-management [Joanna Penn's story about pilgrimage and delayed creative dividends]

SFA 094 – Breaking Six Figures Without Advertising and Reducing the Time It Takes to Revise and Publish (Six Figure Authors podcast, June 10, 2021) https://6figureauthors.com/podcast-player/366/breaking-six-figures-without-advertising-shawn-inmon.mp3 [about "not lying to yourself" and "trusting yourself"]

BOOKS

Cash Flow for Creators by Michael W. Lucas [a.k.a. How to use the "Low Slow Slog" to put yourself in business.] ■

Laurel Decher

GROWTH IN THE INDIE AUTHOR INDUSTRY

I'm about to give the editors of this fine journal a headache. When they gave me the assignment of writing about growth in the Indie Publishing industry, my first thought was "this is a massive subject." The second thought was "I'm gonna need to put 'growth' in quotation marks."

Indie authors didn't just appear on the scene when the iPhone, Kindle, and KDP were introduced in 2007. For years, writers in all genres have published their books and audiobooks without a publishing company.

I'm a fan of Scott Sigler, who released his novel *Earthcore* in 2005 as a serialized podcast after his publisher closed down their imprint (the first in the world, I might add) on Podiobooks.com (now Scribl.com). And Tee Morris even created Podiobooks.com to promote and build an audience for audiobooks without being published, which was a requirement for being on Audible at the time.

And then, thousands of writers like you were out there writing words every day. Some were writing query letters to submit to magazines and publishers. Some were posting their stories to LiveJournal, blogger, and WordPress sites—direct sales and going wide before we had words for them.

In other words, this growth that we see isn't necessarily the result of a platform being available even though it's the largest one on the planet. It's the result of writers like you developing these three aspects of the industry.

GROWTH IN ACCESSIBILITY

Accessibility (noun):
1. the quality of being easy to obtain or use.
2. the quality of being easily understood or appreciated.
3. the quality of being able to be reached or entered.

The ease with which we can produce our stories and send them out in the world is due in part to hundreds of our fellow writers that have created tools that make the work of creating worlds a little more frictionless. Writers have used this momentum to create and publish faster and become better earners.

Imagine that you're on your next book project. You use your plotting software to get the ideas out of your head onto the page and arrange them a bit to resemble a story. From there, you write out your plot. You might even have a program that times your sprints or a website that gamifies the words you write. Or you can use a program that will erase the words if you stop typing. After that, you run it through some software that will correct your spelling and make sure that your editor can read it clearly and has less work to do.

While your manuscript is with the editor, you either buy a few premades (because we all know no one only buys one) or have a few covers made (see the comment on the premades). Or you might check out ad images. (We'll talk about ads more in the next section.)

Once the book is back from your editor, you spend an afternoon formatting the ebook and print versions and then upload it minutes before your preorder is due to begin.

Could you imagine creating your books without Scrivener (launched in 2007), Vellum (launched in 2013), Plottr (launched in 2017), or the army of editors, cover designers, and interior designers?

And the more technology there is, the greater the need to easily find trusted educational sources, and that is the next greatest growth in the indie arena.

GROWTH IN CENTRALIZED EDUCATION

In the early days, it was said that the only folks making money in the indie author industry were the ones making courses teaching people to self-publish. That's a slight exaggeration although there were and are some supposed professionals that want to separate you from your money.

But as writers published more and learned tips and tricks, they were also more willing to share about their experiences on blog posts, forum boards, and podcasts.

Ah, podcasts. Podcasts were my first and most beloved source of information about the industry. The "I Should Be Writing" podcast hosted by author Mur Lafferty has been my top listen since 2005. When I was new to this industry, listening to Mur talk about the struggles and the joys of writing and publishing—before and after Amazon—lit a fire under me.

If "I Should Be Writing" was my weekly inspiration boost, then "Writing Excuses" was my daily dose of craft zen. Released around the same time as "I Should Be Writing," "Writing Excuses" boasts an astounding seventeen seasons of daily fifteen minutes of humor and craft.

The year 2009 brought us "The Creative Penn," and I listened in real time as Joanna Penn built the infrastructure of her business and brought balance to her life at the same time, giving us actionable steps to building a business of our own.

"The Sell More Books Show" landed in 2014, providing commentary on the latest news and trends along with focused and comprehensive bookselling and marketing insights.

From there, we can talk about Jane Friedman who has been a powerhouse in our industry; Johnny, Sean, and Dave of Sterling and Stone; and Mark Dawson of the Self Publishing Formula, which has classes in every aspect of the industry taught by some of the folks previously mentioned.

Not an aspect of our industry doesn't have a high-quality, actionable class, course, or education of some sort behind it.

The digital age has put us in touch with other writers, like-minded souls on the same journey.

GROWTH IN COMMUNITY

Writing and publishing are solitary acts. You look at a computer, battle the blank screen, and chase rogue plotlines and characters that know their own story and don't care about yours.

The digital age has put us in touch with other writers, like-minded souls on the same journey.

That's why the Smarter Artist Summit conference was such a watershed moment. It opened the conference space for not just the authors that were making money but for the ones that wanted to start their journey, the writers (like me) that had a body of work and were paralyzed by the prospect of putting their work out there.

Many of us that went met people we would build empires with. And Smarter Artist Summit gave birth to several conferences, including 20Booksto50K® and The Career Author Summit. ◼

Carishaun Keller-Hanna

From the Stacks

Courtesy of IndieAuthorTools.com
Got a book you love and want to share with us?
Submit a book at IndieAuthorTools.com

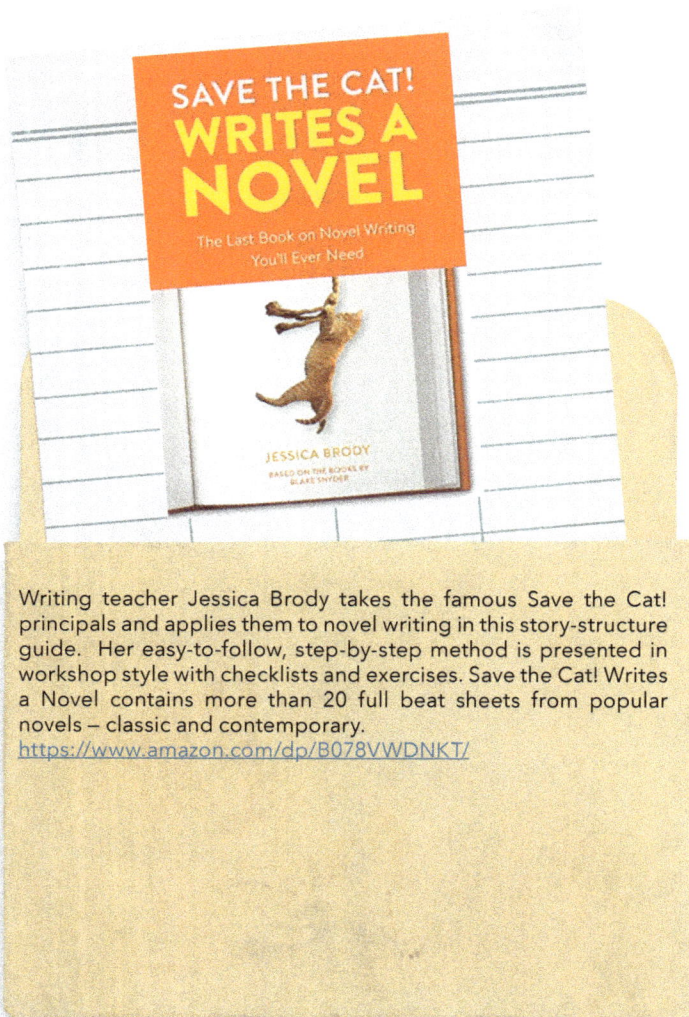

Writing teacher Jessica Brody takes the famous Save the Cat! principals and applies them to novel writing in this story-structure guide. Her easy-to-follow, step-by-step method is presented in workshop style with checklists and exercises. Save the Cat! Writes a Novel contains more than 20 full beat sheets from popular novels – classic and contemporary.
https://www.amazon.com/dp/B078VWDNKT/

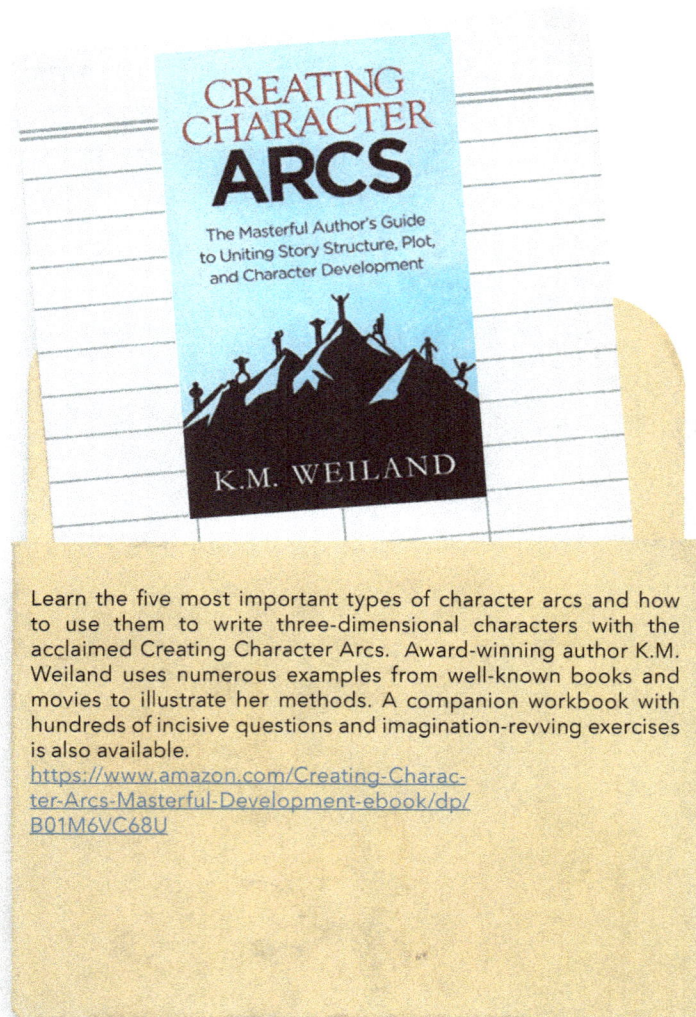

Learn the five most important types of character arcs and how to use them to write three-dimensional characters with the acclaimed Creating Character Arcs. Award-winning author K.M. Weiland uses numerous examples from well-known books and movies to illustrate her methods. A companion workbook with hundreds of incisive questions and imagination-revving exercises is also available.
https://www.amazon.com/Creating-Charac-ter-Arcs-Masterful-Development-ebook/dp/B01M6VC68U

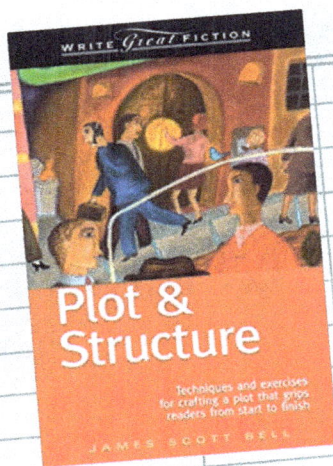

In Write Great Fiction: Plot & Structure, James Scott Bell offers clear guidance to help you create a memorable plot. He covers story structure models and methods for numerous genres. You'll find exercises at the end of each chapter and tools and tips for fixing common plot problems. This concise guide is chock-full of detailed checklists, plot examples taken from well-known novels, and practical advice.
https://www.amazon.com/dp/B001UISGV6/

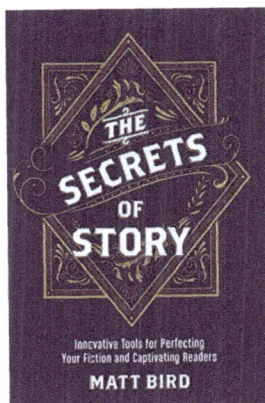

In The Secrets of Story, Matt Bird shares his insights on story structure. The book focuses on what Bird calls the seven skills of writing: concept, character, structure, scene work, dialogue, tone, and theme. His Ultimate Story Checklist helps you hone all aspects of your manuscript. If you want to know what makes a great story work, this is a worthy addition to your toolkit.
https://www.amazon.com/Secrets-Story-Innovative-Perfecting-Captivating-ebook/dp/B01N7HV0CT/

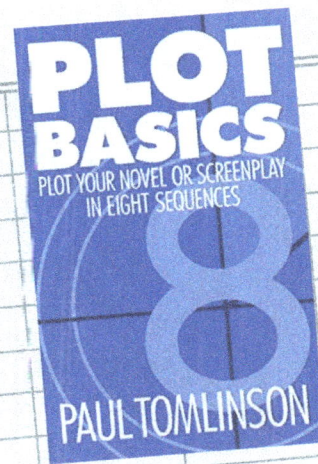

In Plot Basics, Paul Tomlinson shares the pattern he uses to create novels in multiple genres. "A handful of plot points placed in the correct order" will give you a story that readers find satisfying, according to the British author. In this concise how-to guide, he explores the genesis of the eight-sequence plot model, its value to writers, and how to use the method in different popular genres.
https://www.amazon.com/Plot-Basics-Novel-Screenplay-Sequences-ebook/dp/B075FFMDDQ

AUTHOR·TECH·SUMMIT

Summer, 2022
AuthorTechSummit.com

INDIE AUTHOR NEWS & EVENTS

For the latest on news and events pertinent to the indie author community, please check out our interactive calendar here:

Got news or events to share with the Indie Author Community? Let us know at news@indieauthormagazine.com.

In This Issue

Executive Team

Chelle Honiker, Publisher

As the publisher of Indie Author Magazine, Chelle Honiker brings nearly three decades of startup, technology, training, and executive leadership experience to the role. She's a serial entrepreneur, founding and selling multiple successful companies including a training development company, travel agency, website design and hosting firm, a digital marketing consultancy, and a wedding planning firm. She's organized and curated multiple TEDx events and hired to assist other nonprofit organizations as a fractional executive, including The Travel Institute and The Freelance Association.

As a writer, speaker, and trainer she believes in the power of words and their ability to heal, inspire, incite, and motivate. Her greatest inspiration is her daughters, Kelsea and Cathryn, who tolerate her tendency to run away from home to play with her friends around the world for months at a time. It's said she could run a small country with just the contents of her backpack.

Alice Briggs, Creative Director

As the creative director of Indie Author Magazine, Alice Briggs utilizes her more than three decades of artistic exploration and expression, business startup adventures, and leadership skills. A serial entrepreneur, she has started several successful businesses. She brings her experience in creative direction, magazine layout and design, and graphic design in and outside of the indie author community to her role.

With a masters of science in Occupational Therapy, she has a broad skill set and uses it to assist others in achieving their desired goals. As a writer, teacher, healer, and artist, she loves to see people accomplish all they desire. She's excited to see how IAM will encourage many authors to succeed in whatever way they choose. She hopes to meet many of you in various places around the world once her passport is back in use.

Writers

Angela Archer

Having worked as a mental health nurse for many years, Angela combines her love of words with her love of human psychology to work as a copywriter in the UK. She independently published a novella and novel in 2020 and is currently fending off the lure of shiny new novel ideas to complete the second book in her sci-fi series.

When she's not tinkering with words, she's usually drinking tea, playing the saxophone (badly), or being mum and wife to her husband and two boys.

Elaine Bateman

In her pre-author life, Elaine worked for FTSE 100 and Fortune 500 companies in procurement, project support, and IT Training. She has a bachelor of scienceBSc. in Systems Practice and Design.

She is the author of eight published fiction novels and is working on her ninth.

Elaine enjoys giving back to the writing

community through her work with 20Booksto50k, an online author community.

She was the Acorn Sports Bar Ladies' Yard-of-Ale Speed-drinking champion of 1985 (she was the only lady to enter and it took her all night.)

She lives in the UK with her husband, son, and three dogs. She no longer drinks ale.

Laurel Decher

There might be no frigate like a book, but publishing can feel like a voyage on the H.M.S. Surprise. There's always a twist and there's never a moment to lose.

Laurel's mission is to help you make the most of today's opportunities. She's a strategic problem-solver, tool collector, and co-inventor of the "you never know" theory of publishing.

As an epidemiologist, she studied factors that help babies and toddlers thrive. Now she writes books for children ages nine to twelve about finding more magic in life. She's a member of the Society for Children's Book Writers and Illustrators (SCBWI), has various advanced degrees, and a tendency to smuggle vegetables into storylines.

Greg R. Fishbone

Greg R. Fishbone is an author of science fiction and mythic fantasy for young readers including the Galaxy Games series of middle grade novels and the mythic fantasy serial, *Becoming Hercules*. Greg is the founder of Mythoversal, a project dedicated to broadening representation in classical tales by amplifying historically marginalized identities and restoring traditions erased by centuries of gatekeeping. As a former Assistant Regional Advisor for the Society of Children's Book Writers and Illustrators, Greg co-directed regional conferences for authors and illustrators and presented workshops on a variety of craft and career development topics. He also served as president of the groundbreaking Class of 2k7 group of debut authors.

Chrishaun Keller-Hanna

Chrishaun Keller-Hanna is an award-winning journalist, teacher, technical writer, and fiction author that lives for explaining difficult concepts in a way that non-technical readers can understand.

She spent twenty years teaching literacy and composition to a variety of students from kindergarten to college level and writing technical documentation for several tech companies in the Austin area. At the age of forty-three, she decided to write fiction and has published over thirty titles so far with plans to extend out to comics and board games.

When she's not writing, she's traveling, playing video games, or watching movies. When she's not doing THAT, she's talking about them with her husband and grown daughters.

Marion Hermannsen

Marion is a bilingual author, working in both German and English. She holds a master of arts in English, Spanish, and Italian, as well as a diploma of marketing. She spent thirteen years both in London and Ireland while working in the finance and consulting industry.

Marion loves learning about writing craft and marketing best practices. She spends time mentoring other writers and enjoys the freedom of being able to work from anywhere.

She now lives in Frankfurt and is an active member of the local writing community, having published nine novels to date.

Her Irish husband has not only taught her the benefits of drinking copious amounts of black tea, but has impressed his Irish accent on her, to the amusement of her friends and colleagues.

Angie Martin

Award-winning author Angie Martin has spent over a decade mentoring and helping new and experienced authors as they prepare to send their babies into the world. She relies on her criminal justice background and knack for researching the tiniest of details to assist others when crafting their own novels. She has given countless speeches in various aspects of writing, including creating characters, self-publishing, and writing supernatural and paranormal. She also assisted in leading a popular California writers' group, which organized several book signings for local authors. In addition to having experience in film, she created the first interactive murder mystery on Clubhouse and writes and directs each episode. Angie now resides in rural Tennessee, where she continues to help authors around the world in every stage of publication while writing her own thriller and horror books, as well as branching out into new genres.

Susan Odev

Susan has banked over three decades of work experience in the fields of personal and organizational development, being a freelance corporate trainer and consultant alongside holding down "real" jobs for over twenty-five years. Specializing in entrepreneurial mindsets, she has written several non-fiction business books, once gaining a coveted Amazon #1 best seller tag in business and entrepreneurship, an accolade she now strives to emulate with her fiction.

Currently working on her fifth novel, under a top secret pen name, the craft and marketing aspects of being a successful indie author equally fascinate and terrify her.

A lover of history with a criminal record collection, Susan lives in a retro orange and avocado world. Once described by a colleague as being an "onion," Susan has many layers, as have ogres (according to Shrek). She would like to think this makes her cool, her teenage children just think she's embarrassing.

Clare Sager

Holding two degrees in creative writing, Clare Sager is an author of steamy Romantic Fantasy and Fantasy Romance, as well as an editor and outline coach. She's based in Nottingham, UK, where she collects fountain pens, lifts weights, and will fight anyone who dares question the place of romance in fantasy stories (or at least give them a stern talking to). She likes cats, coffee, and speaks fluent sarcasm.

Nicole Schroeder

Nicole is a storyteller at heart. A journalist, author, and editor from Columbia, Missouri, she delights in any opportunity to shape her own stories or help others do the same. Graduating with a bachelor's degree from the Missouri School of Journalism and minors in English and Spanish, she's worked as a copyeditor for a small-town newspaper and as an editor for a local arts and culture magazine. Her creative writing has been published in national literary magazines, and she's helped edit numerous fiction and nonfiction books, including a Holocaust survivor's memoir, alongside international independent publishers. When she's not at her writing desk, Nicole is usually in the saddle, cuddling her guinea pigs, or spending time with family. She loves any excuse to talk about Marvel movies and considers National Novel Writing Month its own holiday.

COME VISIT

the *Cake Machine* STAY for the *Conference.*

Las Vegas
Nevada
November
14-18, 2022

writelink.to/20Books

20 BOOKS
TO 50K®
A RISING TIDE LIFTS ALL BOATS

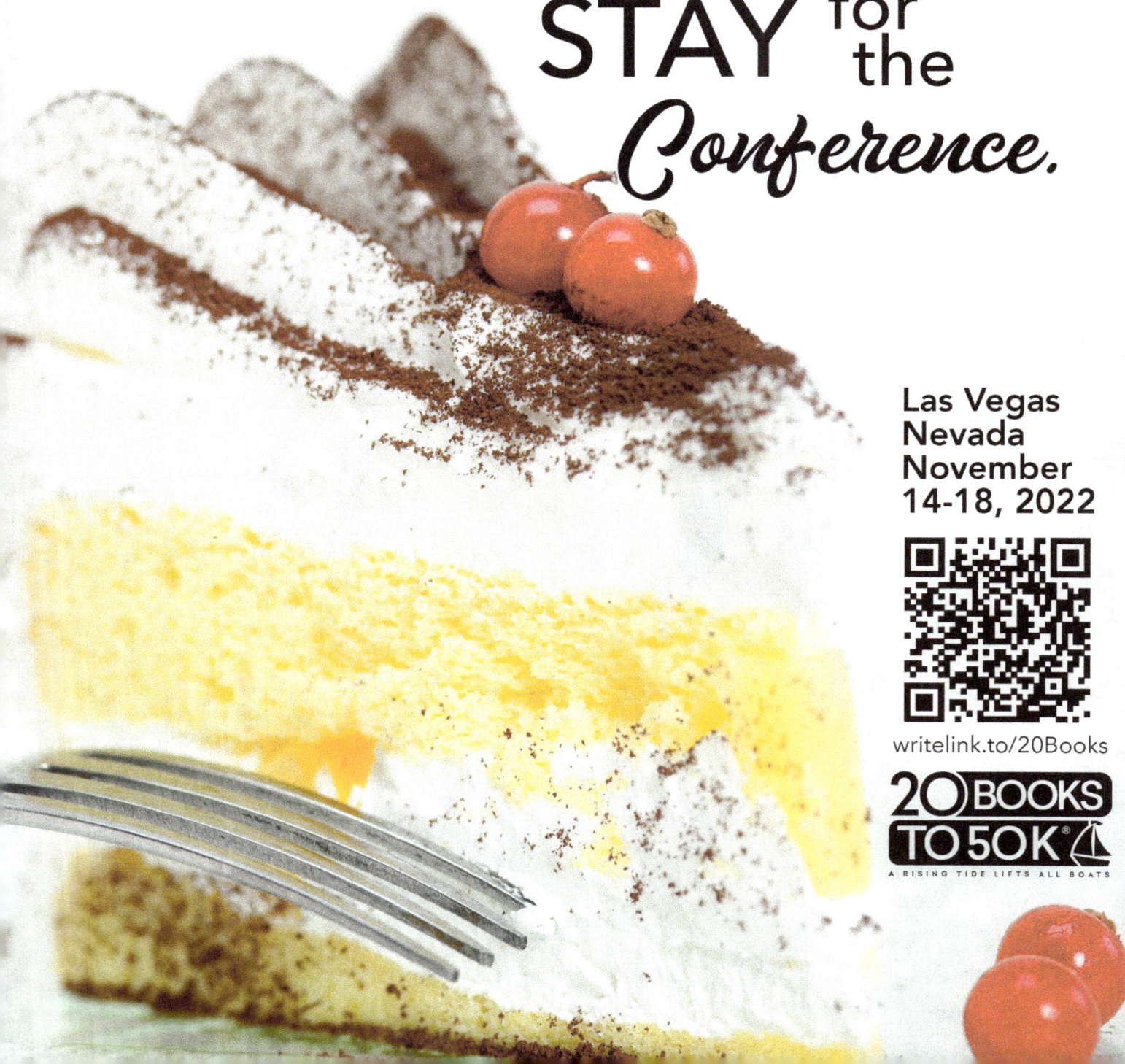

www.ingramcontent.com/pod-product-compliance
Lightning Source LLC
Chambersburg PA
CBHW081748200326
41597CB00024B/4431